PETE TURNER

THE GREAT PHOTOGRAPHER

PETE

Attilio Colomb

TURNER

COLLINS

PETE TURNER

by Attilio Colombo

Pete Turner, photograph by Eric Meola

With some special exceptions, we generally think of photography as an 'occupation'. Those exceptions include the classic photoreporter in the role of witness or with a civil commitment, or the artist photographer who is presumably freed from material pressures. But, today, every professional photographer has precise product requirements and delivery deadlines to meet.

The modern photographer is part of a production process that absorbs him, and exploits (and limits) his professional abilities. Yet even if he is bound up with the big industries—the worlds of advertising, information or consumerism—the photographer always retains a distinct dimension for himself as a craftsman. This is not only because it is the photographer himself who manipulates, at different stages, the elements that go into making an image. He is also in a position to bring in at any moment a wide range of expressional and technical variations that prevent his work from becoming routine.

Every persuasive image—that is to say, every image intended for advertising or commercial use—is strictly related to its purpose, and so to the needs of the client. The client, however, does not have the means to achieve this purpose on his own, and so turns to a specialist: the photographer. This gives the photographer an area of discretion. The more the photographer can add to the initial idea (without succumbing to lapses of taste and creativity!) with proposals and solutions of his own, drawn from his own professional techniques and resources, the greater this discretionary area will be. In fact, the photographer of today is in a similar position to the artist or craftsman of the Middle Ages or the Renaissance commissioned by bishop or prince to decorate a church or palace and thus to instruct the people, enlightening and amazing them with his skill.

In this sphere, photography has progressively supplanted painting or sculpture. The Renaissance prince has been replaced by other princes: the great multinational concerns that require material for their promotional campaigns; private galleries; publishing firms; and public corporations. All, on on different levels, are surrounded by a coterie of artists who daily produce merchandise invariably intended for a specific purpose. Just as in the 16th century artists received precise instructions about how to produce a picture, today photographers receive directly from the client or advertising agency briefs that are at times quite rigid. Much as a photographer may wish to claim autonomy, his product is part of a process to which others, before and after him, contribute their own skills.

This is the type of framework in which Pete Turner, the acclaimed 'wizard of colour', operates. Turner is a recognized master of creative pictures. Yet despite official recognition, he must reckon daily with a clientele which, while satisfied with his original contributions, is always concerned with the function of the 'images' that he is able to supply.

Today Turner is in a position to turn down jobs that are too demeaning or art directors who are either over-demanding or barely willing to cooperate. But it wasn't always like that. His career and his international standing were gradually forged through a relentless quest to uncover the innermost secrets of colour photography.

Born on 30 May 1934 in Albany, New York State, Pete Turner was educated in Montreal in Canada and then Rochester, N.Y. Those were the years when, in the field of photography, America spoke primarily the language of photojournalism. Roy Stryker directed the work of photographers for the Farm Security Administration, and Henry Luce set the wheels in motion of a new illustrated weekly, *Life*. Apart from social journalism, there was artistic photography, which Turner certainly heard them talking about in 1946, when the New York Museum of Modern Art dedicated a grandoise retrospective exhibition to Edward Weston. But as a teenager Pete Turner had a passion for chemistry. Photography attracted him because of the magic that takes place when a picture appears on paper in a darkroom. However, in high school his photography did not go beyond recording occasions: student holidays; groups of graduates receiving their diplomas; and sporting events. Very soon he became the 'class photographer'.

After leaving Montreal for Rochester, he enrolled at the Rochester Institute of Technology. He and his contemporaries were the lucky first to be able to take a Bachelor of Fine Arts course in photography, started only that year in 1952. The photography he learned was still tied to the concept of Fine Art: expressiveness and, above all, absolute control of technique. (Rochester is the core of American photographic technology, the headquarters of the great yellow house, Kodak.) Outside college hours, with American teacher and critic Ralph Hattersley ('A great man', Turner would later say) he was able to frequent museums, galleries and the New York sanctuaries of art. Here he discovered surrealist pictures by Magritte and Tanguy, and his penchant for mystery received decisive momentum. In his final year at college, he made a tour of New York City, visiting the most acclaimed (and disputed) international photographic exposition: Edward Steichen's *The Family of Man*.

In 1956 Pete Turner left the Institute with a BA degree. He further refined his skills by working during summer holidays with a Speed Graphic 4×5 (10× 12.5cm), taking pictures for postcards. Almost immediately he was drafted into the army, and that was where he was able to profit by the second great opportunity of his life. As a photographic specialist, he was transferred to the Pictorial Service Division, the American Army's laboratory of colour photography, on Long Island.

Other photographers in the unit traversed the world to document landings, military exercises, outposts, rocket launchings and manoeuvres. In contrast, Turner spent two years shut up in a laboratory. The young specialist had within his reach all the means and material he wanted—and it was top quality, at times even ahead of that available on the civilian market. He was therefore able, with his taste for manipulation, to give vent to all his fantasies and experimental ideas, trying out the most absurd chromatic variations of colour printing on paper.

In 1958, newly discharged, he threw himself into the heart of the New York of business, magazines and advertising. In those years, alongside the mighty mast-heads of photojournalism (*Life, Look, Time*), fashion magazines were making strides and the advertising market was expanding, gradually becoming more sophisticated. At 24, Pete Turner found his portfolio consisted only of experimental works, undoubtedly original but all achieved 'in private'. For six months, armed with a confidence in his own ability, he made the rounds of all the editorial offices and advertising agencies in New York. 'The art directors flipped when they saw those prints. They had never seen negative prints so rich in colour. This was before 1960, and I really had something to offer.'

Among his visits was one to *Esquire* magazine. Nothing special, they told him; but he was persistent and, at last, Bob Benton accepted him. Turner proposed doing a piece on trains with three pages of notes. The magazine undertook to pay his expenses, nothing more. From that day on, *Esquire's* office began receiving expense bills from every part of America. Finally Turner himself showed up, with the photographs. Fantastic! An exceptional control of colour, a marvellous series,

'The art directors flipped when they saw those prints. They had never seen negative prints so rich in colour.'

eight pages in *Esquire* (his first published work) and Pete Turner was 'in', in the New York that really counts.

From then on, he began to be swamped with work orders: 'Even if I worked 24 hours a day, I'd still have to turn down work,' he claimed. He worked in practically every area of photography: news reporting; advertising cosmetics, airlines, automobiles and a thousand types of commissions; industrial and commercial photography for publishing companies and television networks, film production houses; and so on.

Many of his news story pictures were published in *Look, Holiday, Esquire, Playboy, Time, Life, Sports Illustrated, National Geographic Magazine* and *Omni*. He photographed wild animals, volcanic eruptions, holiday resorts for the jet-set crowd, sports, news items, science, fashion, and industry. Having a yen for sci-fi, he created publicity shots for the film *Close Encounters of the Third Kind* (by Steven Spielberg, with Doug Trumbull, 1978). Many photography journals published his remarkable pictures.

Today, at his well-equipped studio in the Carnegie Building in West 57th Street, New York, with two assistants and a secretary at his beck and call, Turner conjures up memories of the photographer in *Blow-Up*. Antonioni's film represents for him the pace-setting dimension of a photographer's creative freedom. 'In the happenings of the '60s one could get a quick view of life and photograph it. Living is different as a photographer, because a photographer must experience life without stopping, to capture it better on film. Only in this way does he participate in events that go beyond the commonplace.' That's when he is not travelling around the world in a jumbo jet or in Concorde, a can of Pepsi-Cola forever in his hands, looking for subjects that he needs to flesh out the idea of the moment. Or when he is not immersed in the peace of his country home.

Pete Turner's photography certainly has its place in the creative realm. It is a continuous, complex and very rich invention of images—for Turner maintains that the value of the photographic process consists not so much in reproducing reality, as in creating from the new another reality. He was deeply disturbed by reading, back in the '50s, Henri Cartier-Bresson's book *Images à la sauvette* (literally 'surreptitious images'; published in English as *The Decisive Moment*). The theories of the French photographer, particularly that of the 'decisive moment', overturned his convictions, casting a doubt on his method of working. From that time, he always sought to exorcize the fascination of the real world: 'Reality continues to put obstacles in my way.'

The bedrock principle on which Turner has built his entire work is this: 'It is hard to take pictures, but I want to get another reality in my photography, or more reality.' It is a question, of course, of just what is meant by 'more reality'.

Playing on symbols, at times on elementary illusions—a geometric shape, a dominant colour, a juxtaposition or association of ideas—on subconscious relations, on a synthesis of psychic automatisms, on the attempted rationalization of nightmares or of the absurd, Turner's photography springs from the imagination. He has the capacity to visualize the ultimate solution in the midst of an undecipherable chaos.

In a famous sonnet, Michaelangelo wrote:
> 'The finest artist has no idea
> which marble alone in itself does not circumscribe . . .
> . . . and only to that reaches out
> the hand that obeys the intellect.'

'Living is different as a photographer, because a photographer must experience life without stopping, to capture it better on film.'

From Michaelangelo's 'marble' (that is, from the shadows that obscure the picture) Turner manages to obtain his results with impressive technical mastery.

We shall see on the following pages the technical and mental approaches through which this takes place. What counts, for now, is to stress how very rich in effects Turner's photography is. Almost always a pleasure when it is not disturbing, and immediately understandable, it is founded on the decisiveness of the means used (a photograph 'cannot lie' in the common phrase) and is functional enough to prove decidedly the thesis that he wishes to uphold. If we look closely at it, it is not at all a thesis (at least in the terms of logical rationality to which Western tradition has accustomed us) because the pictures of Pete Turner do not address the individual's reason but his emotions, feelings and affective reactions, through the subconscious and the irrational.

The essential purpose of this photography, which I have defined elsewhere as persuasive, is to create a desire that is all the more intense and productive, the less it can be analyzed by cold reason. To arrive at this, Turner uses a well-supplied arsenal of expressive instruments. First among them is colour, enhanced by his technical insights which bring it to the fore and make it the main ingredient of his unmistakable style. Together with a few others, such as Jay Maisel, Ernst Haas and Art Kane, Pete Turner is a fully fledged member of that small New York-based circle of masters of colour photography.

But, besides the almost wizardlike mastery of a continually reinvented colour, Turner has other arrows to his bow. He never puts forward what he represents; he binds it to concepts, situations, and ideas associated with the scale of values of the group for whom the picture is intended. Turner sells suggestions obtained through a wide use of metaphor, allegory, stereotype, symbol, emphasis, paradox: even in pictures like that of the volcano of Iceland, where the coloured spectre that threatens a small town crouched at its feet evokes ghostly visions of sci-fi reverie (pages 52–53). Or in those of animals, where the monochromatic quality obtained by special filters strips away the informative value of the picture, to replace it in full with emotional value only (pages 19, 20–21, 22 and 23).

According to picture editor John Durniak, who has written at length about him, Turner is an orderly man, who reluctantly admits the intrusion of happenstance in his world. But the world he wants to organize absolutely is that which he incessantly invents and creates. For him, as for a good number of American photographers, the photograph is not a fragment of reality belonging to him who can capture it at the right moment. Rather, it belongs to him who knows how to meditate on it at length, and unearth it amid contradictory signs. Typical is the episode of the trash can on the Florida beach (page 43). Turner noticed the bin that had just been placed on the beach; he took it and placed it in the spot most suitable for the shot he had in mind. Then he took a picture. 'What did I do wrong with this photo?' he would later say. 'Nothing, I believe. I am constantly surprised at how many photographers refuse to manipulate reality, as though this were wrong. Change reality! If you don't find it, invent it!'

It is no accident that Turner, an avid reader, is also a fan of science fiction. His settings and his atmosphere very much bring to mind from close up (through the technical tightrope walking of reshooting and reproducing) the world beyond. 'Pioneer (the spacecraft) and its photographs from Jupiter and its satellites,' says Turner, 'are a magnificent visual lesson.' And he argues that, beyond earth's atmosphere and out in interplanetary space, there are pictures of great beauty and charm to be captured and enlivened.

Besides the almost wizardlike mastery of a continually reinvented colour, Turner has other arrows to his bow . . .

But until he is able to climb aboard a spaceship and photograph the splendours of the starry universe, Pete Turner prefers to create in the laboratory his invisible worlds, pictures 'with the flavour of the future, that create colour effects, that call up science fiction and are projected into space'.

Although it could be argued that the force of Pete Turner's pictures has nothing to do with the logic of their construction, so immediate is their emotional reading, it is useful to check the methods by which he devises his own distinctive style. Turner, more than other colour photographers, depends on the manipulation of the basic photographic principles for his effects. The photographer himself admits, 'I don't change colours just to try them out, but I do what I can so that they will work for me.' There is a widespread opinion that a commercial photographer can never be as creative as one who does his work free from incidental concerns. But Turner has proved that it is possible to be creative while adhering to the conditions of an assignment. 'What excites me most about a business commission is that we are dealing with a tremendously consistent subject matter. It is a sort of contest in which you constantly have to keep in shape by working with your mind, and using techniques which you must keep improving on.'

All the moving about required to find the right environment or subject for the best creative opportunities is also in line with commercial work. It may happen that Turner has to go to Central America for a job on shoes. Once there he comes upon a large outdoor theatre, all lit up with dazzling neon lights, which stimulates his fantasy and makes his imagination run riot. Turner confesses that his best opportunities for creative photographs occurred when he was travelling the world for *National Geographic Magazine, Holiday* and *Esquire*.

From the very beginning, Turner was always interested in altering pictures. From a simple embellishment of pictures already existing—that reality which continually set road blocks in front of him—he went on to build images whose existence and value were possible because of a whole series of very individual modifications. He controlled not only the physical appearance, the graphics and the balancing of the composition, but even the chromatic quality with all its tones. Now, using colours, he does what he wants. He states that it is never his intention to go to extremes: 'The difference between gaudy colours and a gaudy use of any particular colour can be enormous.'

'The difference between gaudy colours and a gaudy use of any particular colour can be enormous.'

While in the '60s Turner's skies became orange and his grass turned blue, thanks to the use of special filters or infra-red film, today orange skies, blue grass, a street or mountains also appear where they never existed in the original scene. Today his work is certainly more planned out, but he has not lost any freshness or, above all, his capacity to amaze with every new picture.

The elements that appear in Turner's photography are almost always of a basic, stylized form. The picture is always constructed by bringing together very few elements. His surreal worlds—enormous moons lowering over ice structures, geometric solids fluctuating between the clouds of a dark sky, disquieting universes of science fantasy—do not seek a particular logic. The photographer treats them as absurd stereotypes, the inventing of which always plays on the subconscious. In his latest works especially—a universe of rigorously stylized shapes and volumes, which turns the traditional vision of the world upside down—there is a risk of falling into a spectacular kind of superficiality. Turner sidesteps the risk by setting before us pictures that are diverting, disconcerting, and always well done.

continued on page 59

8

THE
PHOTOGRAPHS

Rolling ball, Sudan, 1959

Shapes of things to come, Studio, 1969

Zimbabwe tree, Zimbabwe, 1959

'Cancun bird,' Cancun Peninsular, Mexico, 1981

Liqueurs, Studio, 1965

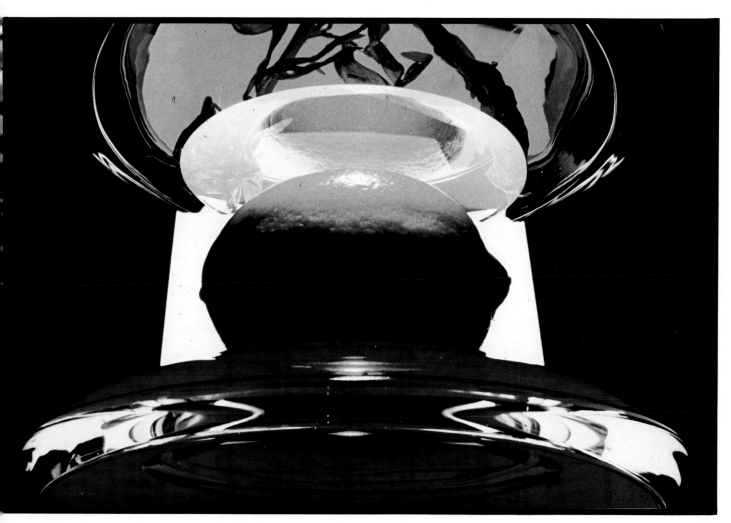

Lemon and oil, Studio, 1967

Soap bubble, Studio, 1979

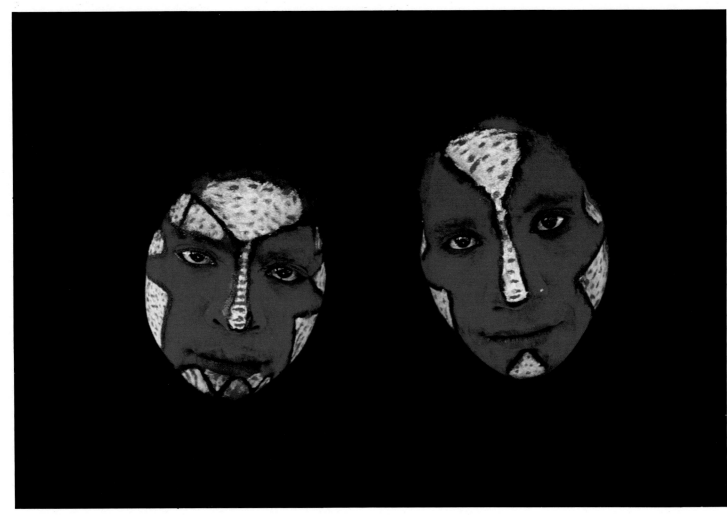

Twins, New Guinea, 1967

Giraffe, Kenya, 1964

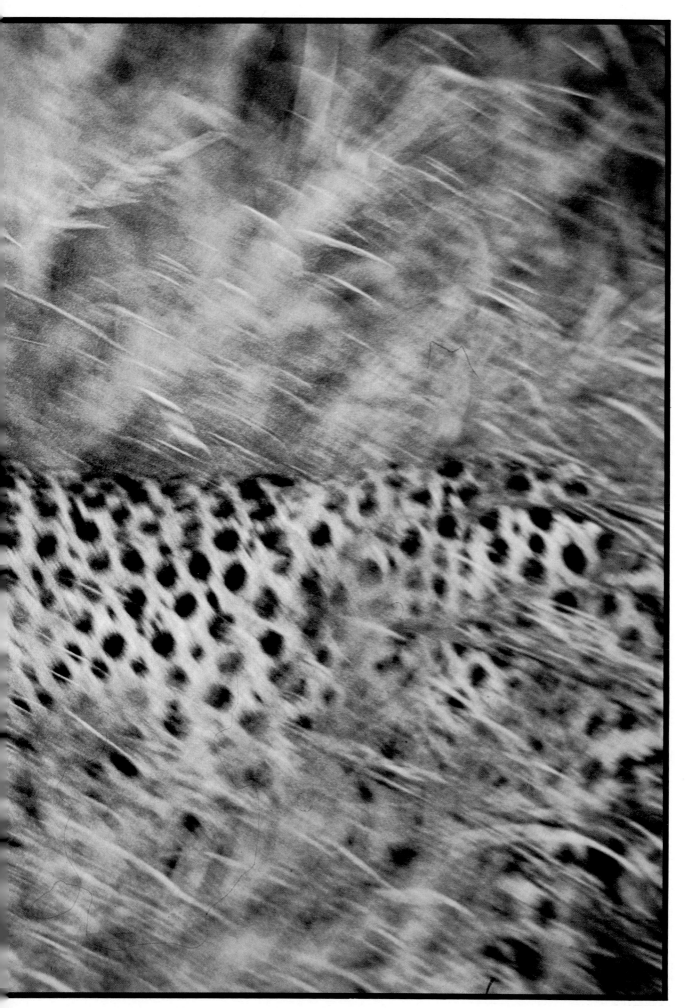

Cheetah, Kenya, 1970

Blue horse, Montana, 1961

Necking, South Africa, 1971

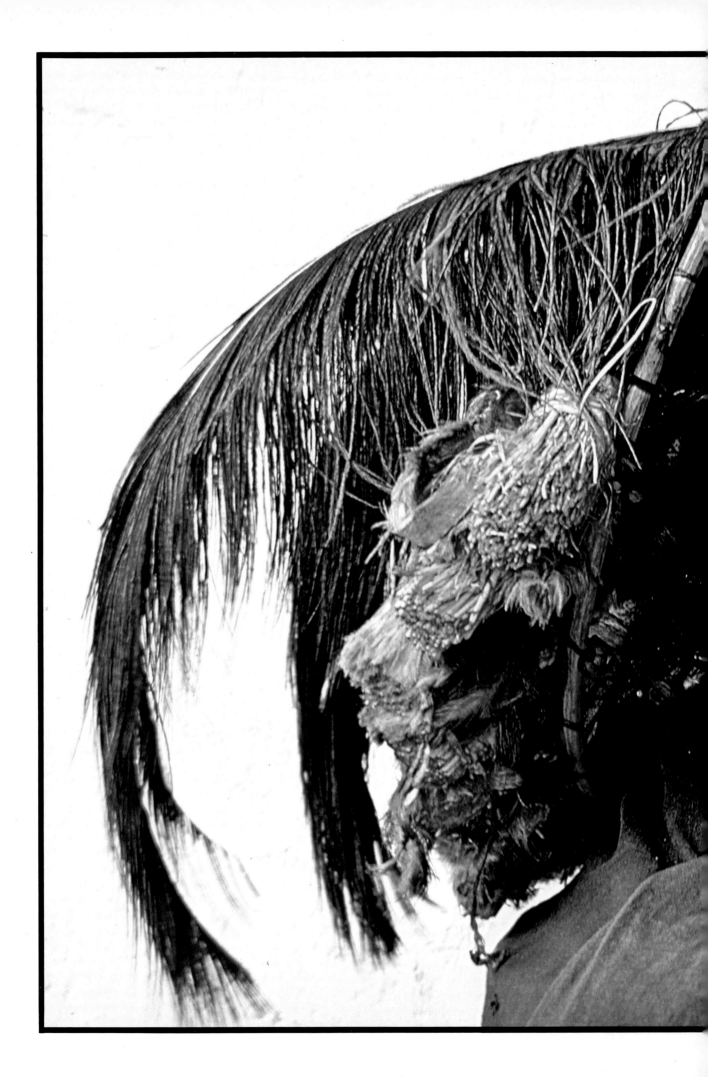

Electric earring, Kenya, 1970

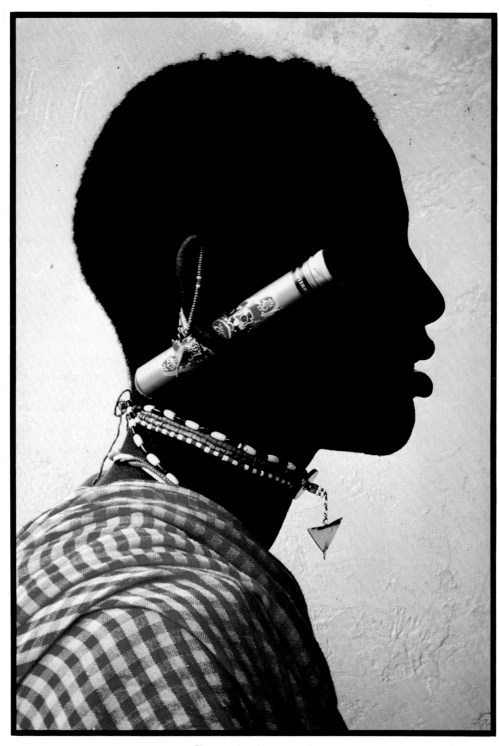

Cigar earring, Kenya, 1970

Tin can earring, Kenya, 1970

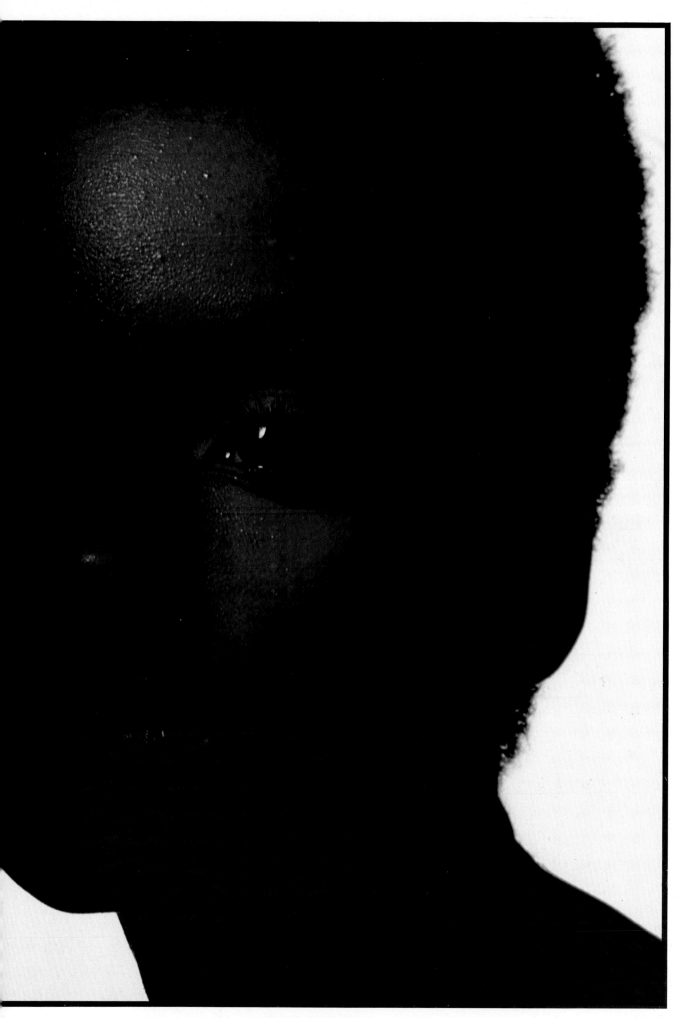

Feelings, Studio, 1968

Sphinx and Moon, Egypt, 1975

Pyramid and Moon, Egypt, 1975

Easter Island, Chile, 1982

Stonehenge, England, 1980

Venice, 1973

Cannonballs, Mozambique, 1971

Road Song, Kansas, 1967

On the railroad, USA, 1981

Truck stop, Utah, 1974

Push, Florida, 1970

Jungle women, Dominica, 1976

Flying women, Dominica, 1976

Man, Utah, 1969

Woman, California, 1974

Hot legs, Studio, 1972

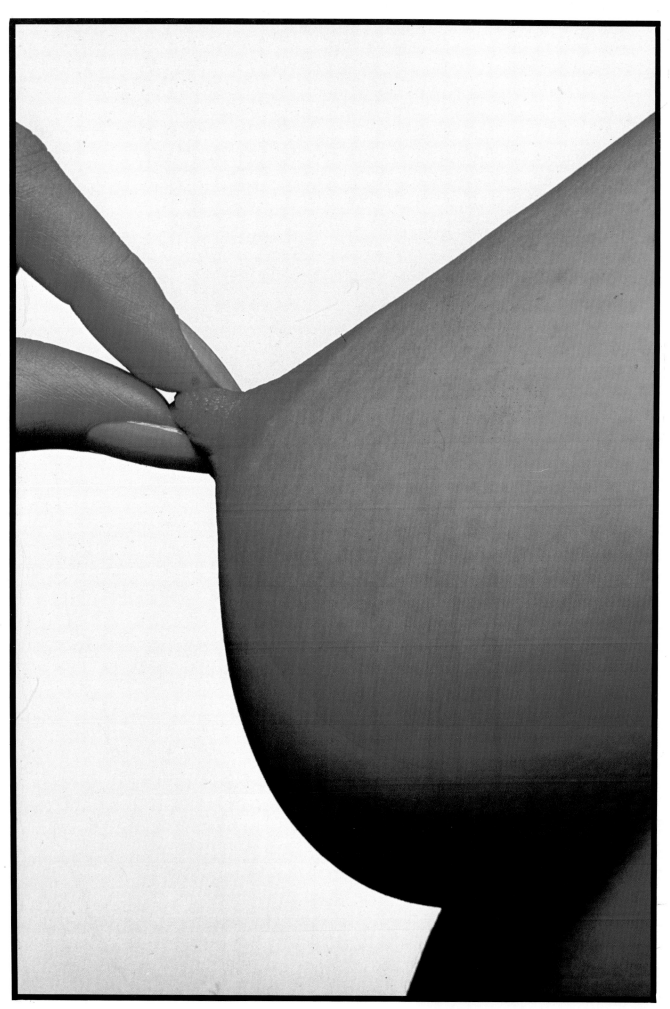

Hot fingers, Studio, 1972

Woman in the tree, Sweden, 1968

Old age, Sweden, 1968

New dawn, Iceland, 1973 (following pages)

Shape of roads to come, USA, 1971

Brazilia, Brazil, 1978

New manscape, Utah, 1969

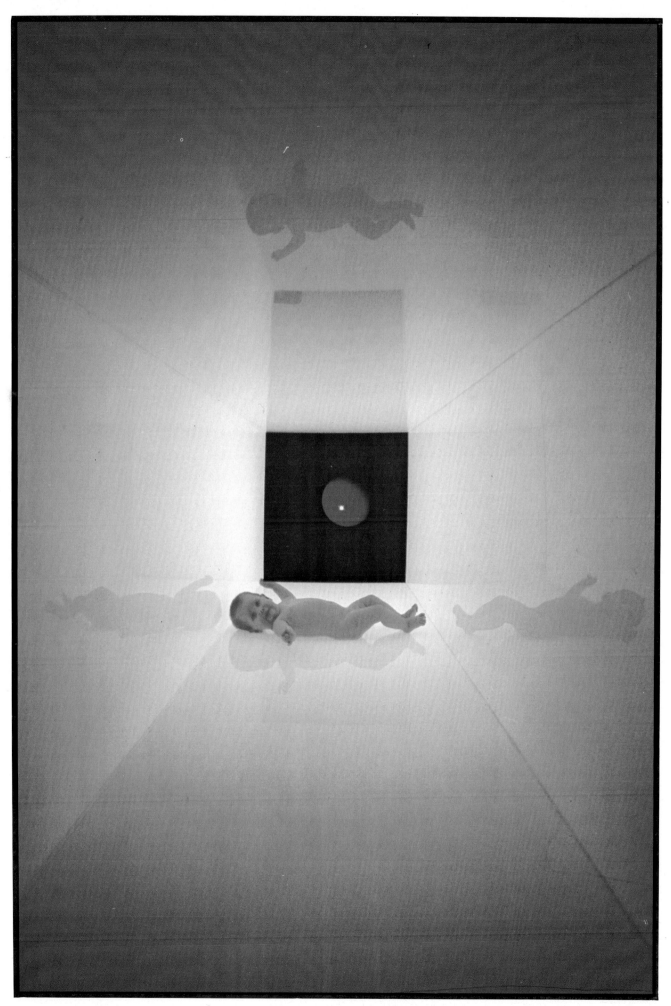

Baby and the sphere, Studio, 1974

continued from page 8

If colour is central to Turner's style, one characteristic of this colour is the absolute lack of nuance, the constant presence of strong and decisive hues. It is basically the sublimation of what is required in a commercial picture. Advertising has no need of nuances, subtleties, distinctions. The advertising message, of which photography is a supporting element and primary in impact, is direct, precise, aimed at the target. Analogously, Turner's colour images, extremely 'simple' from a graphic standpoint, seem to be made precisely to accommodate the desires of an art director. The photographer himself confesses that he feels he is not only a photographer but often wears an art director's hat: 'I always think how my pictures can be used best in a layout, even while I am making them.'

'My method of making photographs resembles science fiction. I am an extra-terrestrial being who lands on a planet that he does not know.' He sees the history of colour photography as nothing but the chronological sequence of modern technology. 'Perhaps we will witness the birth of a new system, in which hitherto unknown pigments will give to a picture hues that are unexpected, rich, stable and long lasting.' Someone defined him as a 'beatnick' of photography, because he consciously violates a large part of the technical taboos. If that's the case, he is a disciplined beatnick, because his purpose in working is to reorder the world and obtain precise results.

His extensive and useful schooling in the colour laboratory of the army taught him all the tricks of the trade, even how to deviate in the use of materials: faded films, material for daylight exposed with studio lamps, films for artificial light used outdoors, utilizing the overall orange mask of a colour negative, mixing two types of brightness (for instance, photographing outdoors with neon light reflections). On the other hand, he always measures exposure with great precision and then usually underexposes a stop, to increase colour saturation.

Notwithstanding the extreme variety of possibilities offered him by technology, Turner prefers standard equipment. He uses Nikon 35mm cameras, and has a wide range of lenses, from 15mm wide angle to the 800mm. But he almost always uses the wide angle: 'My eyesight corresponds to the focal length of 20mm. I can't see, as is normal, at 50mm. I have an enlarged vision, which takes in the edges and expands at the corners. Perhaps it is a defect. I personally think it is a good thing.'

With films too, although he has experimented with many types, he selected ordinary Kodachrome as his choice: he uses it during both shooting and duplication. Perhaps out of love of a challenge, he has also experimented with Polaroid instant film. At Dominica in the Caribbean, with the collaboration of two professional models, he indulged his whim (he had 100 film packs) by taking pictures in the setting of a lush natural environment, on the beach, in a forest, unexpectedly thrilled by the possibility of immediacy, but always keying his pictures to the presence of two to three basic colours, or else to the monochrome obtained when photographing at sunset (pages 44 and 45). But he came right back to Kodachrome, because instant film is ill-suited to his needs as a manipulator. In the same way he rejected Ektachrome. Kodachrome, he says, has the fullest colours that one could desire, it is practically grainless and, above all, it is quite stable chemically: 'I have some Ektachrome material from the '50s which has almost completely changed colours, all green. With the Kodachrome of the same period, however, the colours are still extremely vivid.' If at times he has to shoot in Ektachrome, he later reproduces and duplicates all the material on the more stable

'My method of making photographs resembles science fiction. I am an extra-terrestrial being who lands on a planet that he does not know.'

Kodachrome film. After that, he puts the originals in a bank vault and issues only duplicates through Image Bank, the picture agency.

All his work is based on an initial idea. At times the idea is born complete. It is then a case of getting pictures that manage to give it form. He has just a few favourite subjects and, if need be, he is prepared to travel around the world to find them. The triangular form of the pyramids of Egypt intrigued him for a long time, as did the possibility of defying the force of gravity with spheres. Geometric shapes, exotic animals, sand, water, clouds, sun and moon, and very simple, graphically appropriate landscapes: these are Turner's subjects. His works are abstractions in which, disconcertingly, we rarely find the presence of man.

In any case, taking the picture is only a first step. 'When I am at work making pictures,' he says, 'I first try to photograph the subject from the best point of view, then I begin my search. I consider the essential colours and I wonder whether I can improve on them. If I get an idea in my head that I can immediately make real by making a picture, I experiment with that idea. If it is not possible to modify the colour at the moment of exposure, I photograph on Kodachrome and make all my manipulations later on the optical printer.'

In the shooting stage, to concentrate the colour, Turner almost always uses extremely reduced framing, taking in a particular object—the eyes of a native in New Guinea, a tattoo on someone's chest, the peak of a pyramid. At other times, when the picture is filled with colour, he addresses basic geometric shapes.

But the key phase of Turner's creative process comes in copying. 'I photograph with the optical printer in mind,' he says. Always using Kodachrome film, he copies the original picture several times by means of the optical printer. This is in its crudest form an instrument for duplicating slides, but the machine is essential to Turner's method. 'While the Nikon helps him conceive the picture', wrote someone, 'the optical printer is the instrument that definitively brings it forth. He variously filters, masks, removes, adds, intensifies, inverts, and touches up the original which, little by little, reaches its final form.' Turner pushes the contrast and intensity of the colours to a maximum. His optical printer, which he has personalized by adding filters and instruments he has created, allows him, he says, to create many options. Furthermore, it is equipped with a slide holder that enables the original transparency to be positioned with great precision to within a fraction of a millimetre. This enables him to achieve perfect alignment of two or more pictures when they are being combined. Thus he can transport a Nevada road on to the background of a chain of mountains, recreating a landscape that exists only in his mind; or give the *Woman in the Tree* a head of hair that is a veritable network of leaves (page 50); or open, in homage to Magritte, a window amid the clouds.

Turner's works are essays in metaphor, which the photographer customarily gives titles to, at times on the immediate suggestion of a story that he just finished reading or hearing. 'The title', he says, 'reinforces the reading of the picture.' And it also makes it easier to remember the photograph. Surrealism is, for him, a stylistic instrument, which he uses as long as it allows him to illustrate better the meanings behind things or to put across additional suggestions.

Putting a question to Pete Turner, American photography critic A.D. Coleman raised the hypothesis that, in connection with the visual equivalence of speculative fiction, his work is 'speculative photographic fiction'. There is no doubt that the latest works of the New York photographer are disquieting abstractions. Particularly so are those more directly traceable to sci-fi derivations which, not by chance, have found their way into museum collections in the United States. The relation-

He has just a few favourite subjects and, if need be, he is prepared to travel around the world to find them.

ship between Turner and the galleries has always been characterized by a rather heated dialectic, deriving above all from the unreliability of colour, which in time is subject to change. Today, however, with the introduction of dye-transfer prints that have extremely stable colours, various museums and galleries have begun to take into consideration the possibility of enriching their own collections with Turner's works, which the photographer recognizes as his own only when, having left his hands, they are sealed in guarantee of their artistic quality.

However, to launch his works, even the private ones, Pete Turner has not awaited the decisions of the curators of public or private collections in the United States. Besides the hundreds of pages dedicated to him by magazines, his pictures have travelled the world in numerous exhibitions. And, in New York, they were exhibited at the Space Gallery that Turner, together with Ernst Haas and Jay Maisel, opened in 1976 but which subsequently closed. Turner continues to live and work in New York, exploring new worlds of colour photography and enhancement.

Technical note

If we analyse Pete Turner's pictures to get at their technical core, we find two recurring methods of operation, two formulas. First of all, there is the frequent use of optics of an extreme focal length, with a certain preference for very wide angle lenses. Then there is the manipulation of colours.

The first method, by utilizing the intrinsic features of lenses with a wide field angle, promotes not only the most dramatic use of perspective and hence the picture impact, but also heightens colour intensity. Pete Turner has often expressly stated his preference for working in overcast sky conditions with diffused lighting conditions. More pronounced manipulation of colours and even the realization of monochromatic images are done in very many cases (especially in his more recent works) with the reproduction process at a second stage.

A classic example is the black cannonball that stands out in the centre of blue scenery (page 37). The original slide was taken at dusk, a time of day giving prevalent blue tones which were intensified by placing a medium-blue filter over the lens. To increase the dramatic effect of the scene—an Arab fortress in Mozambique—the picture was then duplicated. Or rather, the original Kodachrome slide was rephotographed full-size in the studio adding further filtration with a light blue filter.

It is interesting to note here that there was no recourse to special duplicating-type films, which are expressly manufactured to keep the contrast of the duplicate identical to that of the original slide. The use of a normal film, but with slow speed and consequently a very fine grain, helped to further heighten the colour contrasts of the scene.

This method of duplicating the original slide, by introducing coloured filters at the time of reproduction, also reduces the risk of vignetting (a fading off of the image at the picture's edges) which is almost unavoidable when filters are placed in front of superwide-angle optics.

An example is the photograph of a fence with the car tail lights on the horizon, taken at dusk with a 20mm superwide-angle lens (pages 38–39).

Pete Turner's duplication interventions have at times been pushed to the most elaborate technical acrobatics. Often pictures resembling those obtained by photographing with film sensitive to infrared rays are in fact the result of repeated duplication. For instance, in some cases Pete Turner has duplicated the original photograph on to reversal (transparency) film but developed the film as though it were a negative film, thus obtaining an inversion of tones and colours. By copying the duplicate obtained with filters of the desired colour, he has arrived at a third picture with chromatic tones entirely different from those of the original.

His still-life photographs of bubbles deserve a separate mention. The technique used to arrive at these fantastic colour tones was more straightforward, although in the desire for perfect results, it was not easy. The colours, in fact, were given by the reflection of coloured panels off-screen on to the bubbles (pages 46–47).

Chronology

1934
Born 30 May in Albany, New York State.

1956
Received degree from the Rochester Institute of Technology.

1957
Worked for the Pictorial Service Division, the colour photo-lab of the American Army, in Long Island, New York.

1958
Settled in New York and went freelance.

1959
Published in *Esquire*—his first feature.

1976
With photographers Ernst Haas and Jay Maisel, he opened the gallery called Space, intended to present colour prints for collectors.

1978
Took the pictures for the publicity of the film *Close Encounters of the Third Kind*.

1979
Held a workshop in Venice.

1981
Received 'Outstanding achievement' award from American Society of Magazine Photographers.

1982
Presenter of 26-part American television series *The Photographer's Eye*.

Bibliography

Major Exhibitions

One-man show at Photokina, Cologne, 1968.
One-man show at George Eastman House, Rochester, N.Y., 1968.
One-man show in Eastman travelling exhibit, 52 countries, 1968–71.
One-man show at Galerie Nikon, Paris, 1976.
One-man show at The Art Institute of Minneapolis, 1976.
One-man show at 'Realisiarte Impressionen', Zurich, 1977.
'The Permanent Color Print', New York Cultural Center of Photography, 1970.

Magazine Features

Popular Photography (USA), August 1959.
Camera 35 (USA), April/May 1962.
Playboy (USA), August 1965.
Popular Photography (USA), March 1967.
Retina (Germany), March 1968.
Photo (Paris), June 1969.
Look (USA), January 1971.
Commercial Photo (Japan), October 1971.
Foto (Stockholm), June/July 1972.
Foto (Germany), September 1972.
Photo (Paris), July 1973.
Photo World (USA), Summer 1973.
Modern Photography Annual (USA), 1973.
Time-Life Photography (USA), 1974.
Photo (Paris), April 1975.
Communication Arts (USA), March/April 1976.
Photo (Paris), September 1976.
Photo (Paris), October 1976.
Photo World (Penthouse) (USA), October/November 1976.
Camera 35 (USA), December 1976.
Zoom (France), January/February 1977.
Photographie (Germany), March 1977.
Mainliner Magazine (USA), August 1978.
Camera 35 Photoworld (USA), August 1978.
Photographer's Forum (USA), August/September 1979.
Foto Magazin (Germany), October 1979.
Il Fotografo (Italy), December 1979.
Il Fotografo (Italy), June 1980.
American Photographer (USA), November 1980.
Studio Photography (USA), January 1981.
Omni (USA), February 1981.
Omni (USA), March 1981.
Today's Photographer (USA), December 1981.
Camera (UK), January 1982.
Nikon World Annual (Japan), 1982.
American Photographer (USA), October 1982.

Index of photographs

Author

Attilio Colombo was born in 1944 near Lake Como in Italy. After graduating from Milan University, he took up photography. He has been editor (and since 1980 editor-in-chief) of *Progresso Fotografico* magazine. He organized exhibitions on 'Japanese Photography of Yesterday and Today' (1979) and 'Photojournalism in Italy' and has edited several monographs on Japanese and Italian photography. He has contributed entries to encyclopedias of photography and writes for several magazines and newspapers in Italy. He also acts as consultant to two Milan art galleries.

First published in 1984 by
William Collins Sons & Co Ltd
London · Glasgow · Sydney
Auckland · Johannesburg

© 1982 Gruppo Editoriale Fabbri S.p.A., Milan

ISBN 0 00 411950 9

Typesetting by Chambers Wallace, London
Printed in Italy